PRAISE FROM DOG EXPERTS

"Darcy Pattison does a remarkable job on several fronts with her wonderful new book *I Want A Dog: My Opinion Essay*. She introduces the value of the written text at an early age to children. This cannot be emphasized enough in our early classrooms. With this comes an important lesson regarding the responsibility of owning and caring for a dog. As President of the Labrador Retriever Club representing the breed with the largest number of dogs I know how imperative responsible dog ownership is and Darcy does a wonderful job instilling this at an early age. This is **a remarkable children's book** that has a lesson."

   –Fred Kampo, President of the Labrador Retriever Club

Other Mims House Books
MimsHouse.com

Wisdom, the Midway Albatross: Surviving the Japanese Tsunami and other Disasters for Over 60 Years. (nonfiction picture book)
   Starred PW review
   2014-15 Sakura Medal Reading List – Children's book award from the English-speaking schools in Japan.

Abayomi, the Brazilian Puma: The True Story of an Orphaned Cub
   (nonfiction picture book)
   2015 National Science Teacher's Association Outstanding Science Trade Book
Saucy and Bubba: A Hansel and Gretel Tale (novel)
The Girl, the Gypsy and the Gargoyle (novel)
Vagabonds: An American Fantasy (novel)
The Aliens, Inc. Chapter Book Series
   Kell, the Alien, Book 1
   Kell and the Horse Apple Parade, Book 2
   Kell and the Giants, Book 3
   Kell and the Detectives, Book 4 (March 2015)

Read Other Books in The Read and Write Series

I Want a Cat: My Opinion Essay
My Crazy Dog: My Narrative Essay (Fall 2015)

MimsHouse.com/newsletter
Get a free ebook - on us!

I Want a Dog:

My Opinion Essay

By Darcy Pattison

Illustrations by
Ewa O'Neill

I Want a Dog: My Opinion Essay

Paperback ISBN 978-1-62944-011-8
Hardcover ISBN 978-1-62944-012-5
eBook ISBN 978-1-62944-013-2

Library of Congress Control Number: 2014913873

Mims House
1309 Broadway
Little Rock, AR 72202
USA
MimsHouse.com

My cousin, Mellie, wants a dog and so do I. We have been emailing about what kind of dog to get. And now, at school, I have to write an essay about the best kind of dog for my family.

Essay is a big word that means you just write about something.
You say it S - A.

My teacher, Mrs. Shirky, says, "Dennis, you have to use criteria."
It sounds like Cry-tear-EE-uh.
(It makes me think about crying tears.)

It means I need reasons for the kind of dog I want.

MY CRITERIA
Big or little?

I want Giant.
Mellie wants Tiny.

Great Dane

Chihuahua

How energetic?
I want a couch potato
who likes to watch TV with me.

 Bulldog

German Shorthaired Pointer

Mellie
wants
a jogger.

Needs exercise!
I am going to love this dog and want to exercise him every day.

Beagle

Mellie is too busy with dance and piano and playing checkers with our Grandma, who moved in at Christmas. She doesn't want to exercise her dog every day.

Yorkshire Terrier

Boxer

Needs lots of play!

I want to play with my dog before
breakfast and all the time after school.
And all day Saturday and Saturday
night and all day Sunday and Sunday night.

Our Grandma
can play with
Mellie's dog
all day long.

Pomeranian

A loving dog?
I want a dog that stays by my side.

German
Shepherd

Poodle

Mellie just wants
a doggie kiss (YUK!)
when she gets home,
and that's enough.

Rottweiler

Other pets?
No other pets.
That's why I want
a dog SO much.

Mellie has had a gerbil, a hamster, and a lizard. But right now, she doesn't have any other pets.

Labrador Retriever

Catch!

Miniature
Schnauzer

Shake!

Easy to train?
Yes! Of course. Duh.
I have lots of tricks
to teach him.

Mellie wants a dog
to do "sit" and
"stay." That's all.

French
Bulldog

A guard dog?
Nope. We don't need that.
Grandma also says, "No."

Cavalier
King Charles
Spaniel

Mellie doesn't mind brushing a dog's coat now and then. She's just too busy to do it every day.

Shih Tzu

Here is my essay:

I Want a Dog

I want a dog. Here are some things I thought about. First, I like big dogs. I want to take him for walks, but I don't want a jumpy dog or a yappy dog. I want my dog to be happy to see me after school. I'll play with my dog before school, after school, and after supper.

I'll teach my dog many things. For example, he will learn to roll over and play dead. Also, he can jump over things or through hoops.

I thought about how the dog would act at home. We don't have any other pets. For example, I don't have cats or hamsters. My dog must be friendly and not growl at other people. Also, I'll love my dog, but I don't want to brush his hair or his teeth.

A

Very good!.

Since I looked at the dog breeds and thought about my criteria, I made a decision. A Bernese Mountain Dog is the best dog for our family. He will be big but not jumpy. He will take walks and stay right with me. He will be smart and learn to shake hands. When the doorbell rings, he will not bark or scare people. My dog and I will be best friends.

I got an A on my essay! And when Mom and Dad read my amazing essay, I got —

— a Bernese Mountain Dog named
Clark Kent!

Mellie got
a Maltese
named
Lois Lane.

Don't tell Mom, but I sneak Clark into the house at night, and he sleeps on my bed. He can already shake hands.

Now, when I get home, I drop my back pack and call, "Clark!" He pokes his head out of his dog house and runs across the back yard and jumps up on my shoulders and licks my face. Doggie kisses. Yuk! (Well, maybe not a big yuk.)

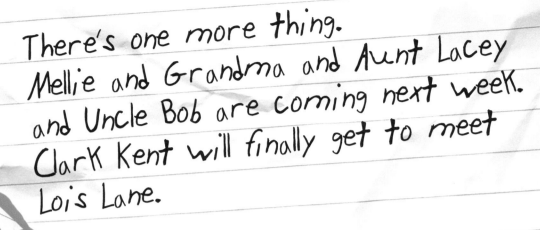

There's one more thing.
Mellie and Grandma and Aunt Lacey
and Uncle Bob are coming next week.
Clark Kent will finally get to meet
Lois Lane.

Writing with Kids about Dogs

How to Choose a Dog
- Shared or Individual Research Project

For a shared or individual research project, AnimalPlanet.com offers an interactive Dog Breed Selector tool (http://www.animalplanet.com/breed-selector/dog-breeds.html), which uses criteria to narrow the choices to a few appropriate breeds. A how-to essay can concentrate on the importance of using criteria to select a dog. This story includes nine criteria: size, energy level, exercise needs, play needs, affectionate, get along with other pets, easy to train, guard dog, and grooming needs. Other criteria might include allergies, weather related issues, family traditions, price, male or female, availability in your area, and specific needs such as a dog trained in duck hunting. Students can choose the most important criteria for their family and write about how to choose the right dog for them.

I Want a Dog - Opinion Essay

This book is a model text for writing an opinion essay about the kind of dog that is best for a family. Students could write Mellie's essay about choosing the Maltese. To write about their own family, students should do prewriting about their criteria or reasons for choosing a certain dog breed.

Dog Breeds - Informative Essay

Use this book as prewriting to help students narrow their focus to just one or two breeds of dogs that interest them. From there, students can research dog breeds at the American Kennel Club (http://www.akc.org/breeds/index.cfm) or in a variety of informational books.

Imagined or Real Narrative

Use this book as a model text for writing a real or imagined narrative about a child or family getting a dog or other pet.

CPSIA information can be obtained
at www.ICGtesting.com
Printed in the USA
LVIC06n0012051215
465431LV00019B/286